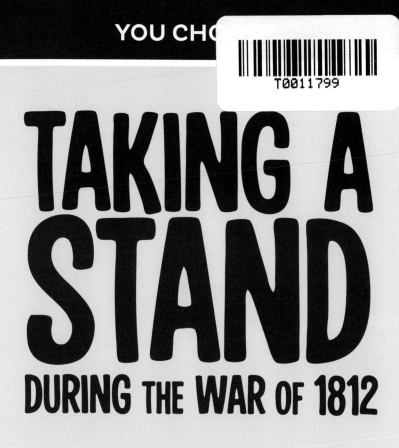

TAKING A STAND

DURING THE WAR OF 1812

A HISTORY SEEKING ADVENTURE

by Matt Doeden

CAPSTONE PRESS
a capstone imprint

Published by You Choose, an imprint of Capstone
1710 Roe Crest Drive, North Mankato, Minnesota 56003
capstonepub.com

Library of Congress Cataloging-in-Publication Data is available on the Library of
Congress website.

ISBN: 9781669032526 (hardcover)
ISBN: 9781669032748 (paperback)
ISBN: 9781669032601 (ebook PDF)

Summary: You have found yourself in the midst of the chaos of the War of 1812
between Great Britain and the young United States. Will you fight in the north on
Lake Erie, or join General Jackson in the south? Or maybe you'll help save precious
items from the White House as the British burn Washington, D.C. Step back in
time to face the challenges and decisions that real people faced during this restless
time in history.

Editorial Credits
Editor: Mandy Robbins; Designer: Heidi Thompson; Media Researcher: Jo Miller;
Production Specialist: Tori Abraham

Image Credits
Alamy: ClassicStock, 30, Everett Collection Historical, 103, FLHC A2020, 71,
Niday Picture Library, 46, North Wind Picture Archives, 4, 33, 84, PS-I, 63, The
Picture Art Collection, 57; Getty Images: Bettmann, 79, John Parrot/Stocktrek
Images, 104, mikroman6, 18, MPI, 76; Library of Congress, Cover, 24, 35, 37;
Shutterstock: Everett Collection, 8, Jon Bilous, 89, Marzolino, 51, Michael Shake,
14, Wally Stemberger, 39; Wikimedia: White House, 99

Printed and bound in the USA. PO5425

TABLE OF CONTENTS

ABOUT YOUR ADVENTURE

YOU are living through a troubled time in American history. The United States won the war for independence from Great Britain in 1783, but tensions between the two countries are on the rise.

When war breaks out in 1812, the balance of power in North America is at stake. The United States wants to expand, while Great Britain seeks to protect its remaining territories. As an American patriot, how will you help in the effort? Will you fight or run? Do you have what it takes to help your nation win the War of 1812?

Turn the page to begin your adventure.

CHAPTER 1

WAR HAS COME

War has come to the United States. Less than 30 years after the young United States of America won independence from Great Britain, the two nations are at war once again. The American Revolution was about independence. This time, the conflict is about territory and economic power. Both sides fear the other becoming too strong. The tension has built, and now war has broken out.

As you walk through the streets, the fighting is all anyone can talk about.

Turn the page.

"The British are letting the American Indians do their fighting for them," says an old woman.

"The Redcoats are nothing but pirates," replies a young man. "They steal our ships and force our men to fight for them."

"President Madison will put an end to this," answers a teenage girl. "I've heard he's gathered militias from every state."

President James Madison

"But we need a proper navy," says the young man. "Britain is crushing us on the seas. If we can build more ships, they won't stand a chance."

The conversations continue as you walk on. Life hasn't been easy for the people of the new nation. The government doesn't have the money for a proper military. Fights with Native peoples in the west are costing lives on both sides.

Great Britain no longer controls the United States. But their economic power still holds an unwelcome influence on the new nation. And Canada is still their territory. The United States was ready to expand, and the British were quick to make sure they didn't expand into Canada.

You're ready to do your part. People of all ethnicities—white, Black, and Native American—are joining up to fight the British and their allies, including you.

Turn the page.

Battle rages in the north, where the British have taken control of the Great Lakes. Native people fight amongst each other and with settlers in the southeast. Meanwhile, British troops even place the nation's capital of Washington, D.C., under threat.

- To be a soldier in the northern United States, turn to page 13.

- To be a Creek scout for the Americans in the southeast, turn to page 45.

- To be an aide to First Lady Dolley Madison during the British attack on Washington, D.C., turn to page 73.

CHAPTER 2

THE PUSH NORTH

The air is still. The waves of Lake Erie lap against the nearby shoreline. Birds circle above.

"It's almost peaceful," says Ezekiel, as the two of you walk to camp. It's the fall of 1813, and the war between the United States and Great Britain has become intense. You look over at your friend and smile. You are white, while Ezekiel is a Black man. Back home, it's a friendship that probably never would have happened. Racism runs strong, even in the northern states. But on the battlefield, a man's skin color doesn't matter to you as long as he has your back.

Turn the page.

You nod. You have lived your whole life in New York. But now you find yourself on the front lines of war, in the wilderness of the young state of Ohio. You never imagined a land so open and beautiful. But you don't let the temporary calm fool you. You're not here for sightseeing.

The shore of Lake Erie in Ohio

You're here to defend the United States, the nation you were born in. You're following in the footsteps of your father, who fought in the American Revolution. He fought for your independence. Now it's your turn to fight.

This time, the British have returned. The Great Lakes, which separate the United States from British-held Canada, are the front lines. British forces control the lakes and have taken U.S. territory along their banks. You'll do all you can to push them back.

As you come into camp, you are struck by how diverse the American forces are. Black, white, and American Indians have all taken up arms for the United States.

And it's not just British redcoats who you're fighting. The enemy forces are as diverse as yours.

Turn the page.

Your commanding officer addresses the troops. "I've spoken with Major General William Henry Harrison. "Our orders are to push north and attack. Our naval forces will take control of Lake Erie. Meanwhile, the general will lead ground forces into Canada. The British have allied with the Shawnee under the leadership of Tecumseh. We will drive them out and regain control of the region."

You glance over at Ezekiel. He's smiling.

"What are you grinning at?" you whisper.

Ezekiel shrugs and says, "Been enlisted three months. It's about time for some real action."

After speaking with your commanding officer in private, you have your orders. It's time to prepare for the fighting.

- To fight with the Navy, go to the next page.
- To march north with the Army, turn to page 20.

You stand on the deck of the USS *Lawrence* as it cuts through the waves of Lake Erie. The ship's twin sails billow above you as the sun filters through hazy clouds.

"Enemy ships ahead," shouts a lookout.

Near the front of the ship, Master Commandant Oliver Hazard Perry stares across the water. The United States' Lake Erie fleet isn't big—just nine ships. But the *Lawrence* is the flagship, and it will be the first into battle. As the sails catch the wind, the *Lawrence* begins to leave the other ships behind.

"Press on," Perry says to you as he watches. You're one of Perry's top officers. He trusts you to make decisions.

Turn the page.

Battle of Lake Erie

As the minutes pass, the British fleet looms ever larger on the horizon. Finally, the boom of a cannon marks the beginning of the battle. The British shot falls far short of the *Lawrence*. But you know that their guns have a longer range than yours.

The ships sail closer . . . closer. Soon, you're within range of the British guns. The ship rocks and shudders as shells slam into its wooden hull.

"We're taking a beating," says one of the sailors as he rushes past you. "I don't know how long the ship can take this."

As if to make his point, another blast rocks the ship, almost knocking you off your feet. The sound rings in your ears. The blast leaves you dazed for a few moments.

Can you keep going like this? Should you try to get closer to get your own guns within range? Or is it time to give the order to return fire, in hopes your guns can reach the British ships already?

- To try to get closer, turn to page 22.
- To return fire, turn to page 31.

You and Ezekiel join your unit's march north into Canada. The fall air is cool, and the trees are just beginning to turn vibrant shades of red, orange, and yellow. The sound of water flowing along the nearby Thames River is relaxing. But you know battle is near.

"Why is he running north anyway?" mumbles John, a fellow soldier. He is referring to Tecumseh, who is leading his confederation of American Indian fighters north. Tecumseh is allied with the British. He has been a thorn in the side of U.S. forces since the war began.

"Our ships broke the British squadron on Lake Erie," Ezekiel replies. "Tecumseh knew that without control of the lake, his advantage was gone. He's going north because it's the only direction he can go."

Ahead of you, Major General William Henry Harrison speaks with several of his officers. You can hear their conversation. " . . . British soldiers forming a line ahead," Harrison says. "Tecumseh is on the flank, ready to attack."

A surge of nervous excitement flows through your body. You've been waiting for a battle. You're about to get it. Harrison plans to send most of his men toward the British line ahead. But he's wary of Tecumseh's men as well—and with good reason. Tecumseh's units have performed well in battle throughout the war. Harrison needs to hold back a side force to fight them off in case they attack.

• To join the main force, turn to page 26.
• To join the side force, turn to page 27.

Firing from this distance would be pointless. Your guns simply don't have the range. "Full ahead," you shout. From afar, Perry nods his approval.

The battle is on. The sound of gunfire fills the air. It's almost constant. The *Lawrence* is hit time and again, but it keeps going. Finally, when you're close enough, you give the order to fire.

The men spring into action, loading and firing the ship's guns. The first few shots miss, but soon you're hitting the British ships.

For several hours, you trade fire. "Where are our other ships?" you ask Perry.

He shakes his head. "We were too far ahead. It's just us against the British fleet."

You don't like these odds, and with good reason. The British continue to pound your ship.

You do as much damage to their fleet as you can. But the outcome is inescapable. The *Lawrence* is going down.

"The USS *Niagara* is coming," Perry says. "We will continue the battle on our sister ship."

It's likely not everyone will make it to the *Niagara*. But Perry must. He is a key officer. Should you make it your duty to ensure he gets there? Or should you stay and fire against the British while the *Lawrence* goes down? Then more of your men could make it to the *Niagara*.

• To transfer Perry to the *Niagara*, turn to page 24.
• To stay with the *Lawrence*, turn to page 34.

The *Lawrence* is going down. All you can do is move Perry to the *Niagara*. It's the same build of ship, so when you step on deck, you feel right at home.

A haze of smoke hangs over the lake. Your ears ring from the constant sound of gunfire.

The USS *Niagara*

Perry looks out at the scene. "We've taken losses, but so have the British," he says.

You nod. "Yes sir."

"We've got a fresh ship and the wind at our backs. We could press forward. If we break through, we could end this battle now."

"Yes sir," you reply again. "It would be dangerous. The British fleet is wounded, but those guns could still tear us apart."

The two of you stand together for several moments. You can tell he's weighing his options. Finally, he turns to you. "What's your advice?" Do you think you should stay back and remain on the defensive?

• To suggest staying back, turn to page 36.
• To suggest attacking, turn to page 34.

You and Ezekiel join the main force. "The British are nearly beaten already," Ezekiel says. "They've been on half rations. They're weak, tired, and ready to give up."

As you march through the Canadian wilderness, gunfire erupts. Ezekiel might be right. But you don't dare underestimate the British troops. A cannon blast strikes a tree not far from your position. You kneel down and prepare to return fire.

"Look there," Ezekiel says, pointing to a cluster of British cannons in a clearing near your position. "They abandoned some of their own cannons in their hurry to retreat. Let's fire them at the British!"

You could do that. But it would be dangerous to cross the clearing. You'd be easy targets for British fire.

- To hold your position, turn to page 29.
- To take the cannons, turn to page 39.

As the main force presses forward, Tecumseh leads his men toward your flank. He's your enemy, but you're in awe of his ability to rally men to his cause and lead them into battle. You march ahead, trying to push them back. But the ground is wet and swampy. You're knee-deep in muck as the fighting breaks out.

"The British line has broken," someone shouts from behind. "They're in full retreat!"

The British may have given up the fight, but Tecumseh's forces aren't giving an inch. In the distance, you catch a glimpse of their famous commander. He commands his troops, even in the face of terrible odds. With the British in retreat, their fight is hopeless.

The battle is slow in the woody swamp. But you carry on, driving the enemy farther and farther back.

Turn the page.

Suddenly, a roar rises among the troops to your right. "We got him!" cries a young soldier, his face covered in mud. "Tecumseh is dead!"

You feel a combination of relief and sadness. The Shawnee leader was your enemy in this war, and his American Indian forces will fall apart without him. But you know in that instant the world has lost an admirable leader.

The moment passes. You've won a victory today, and it will be an important one in the war. You force a smile and celebrate with the rest of the men.

• Turn to page 41.

You shake your head. "No," you reply.

The cannons are on exposed ground.
An enemy could easily see you. Already, the
American line is forcing the British back.
Why take a needless risk? You ignore the
cannons and press forward.

Your boots slosh as you trudge over wet
ground. It's slow going. But the soggy ground
also slows the enemy.

The tired, hungry British troops quickly give
up the fight. After just a few minutes, they're
in full retreat. You help take prisoners, seizing
weapons and securing the area.

The Battle of the Thames is a huge victory.
You spot General Harrison on horseback,
celebrating with his men.

Ezekiel impulsively hugs you.

Turn the page.

"We did it!" he cries. "Our first real battle, and we won!"

You share in his joy, but you can't help but worry about the future. You won a victory today, but you know that it will only get tougher from here. The War of 1812 is far from over.

General Harrison (far right) at the Battle of the Thames

• Turn to page 41.

As you recover from another blast, you give the order. "Fire at will!" you order the crew.

Your men respond swiftly, firing shot after shot in the direction of the British fleet. But your shots fall short. All you're doing is making big splashes.

Sitting here, hopelessly firing, has been a critical mistake. The enemy's guns have more range. Close-in fighting would have been the better strategy.

Another blast rocks the *Lawrence*. The devastating hit blasts a hole in the hull. Water quickly spills inside.

"We're going down!" shouts a sailor.

For a moment, all you can do is stare blankly. The sound of gunfire fills the air like thunder. Your ship is sinking. Nothing can stop that now.

Turn the page.

Finally, you call out the words that make your heart sink. "Abandon ship!"

The rest of the fleet is still coming behind you. The battle is not lost. But your part is over. Your only hope is to be rescued by an American ship.

THE END

To follow another path, turn to page 10.
To learn more about the War of 1812, turn to page 101.

The U.S. fleet in the Battle of Lake Erie

You shake your head. You can't leave your ship.

"I'll stay here and fight," you tell Perry, as he makes his way to a raft.

Even in the chaos of battle, you watch to make sure your commanding officer safely boards the *Niagara*. Then you turn your attention back to the battle.

"We're going to sink, sir," says a sailor. You just nod. You already know that.

"Continue firing," you reply. "We may be going down, but we'll give them everything we have."

As the gunners continue to fire, you help launch as many lifeboats as you can. You get another dozen men to safety before it's too late.

Master Commandant Oliver Hazard Perry

Only a handful of men remain on board when the *Lawrence* finally slips beneath the chilly waters of Lake Erie—yourself included. You've done all you can to help, at the cost of your own life. You only hope that the rest of the fleet makes your sacrifice worthwhile.

THE END

To follow another path, turn to page 10.
To learn more about the War of 1812, turn to page 101.

"We just lost one ship," you say. "Do we really want to risk another one?"

Perry shakes his head. His shoulders slump. You can tell that's not what he wanted you to say. But he agrees.

The battle drags on for hours. The American fleet is outgunned. One by one, your ships fall. Soon, the *Niagara* is the last one left.

"We've lost, sir," you tell Perry. "We have to retreat."

You feel completely beaten and powerless as you turn and flee from the British. You're sure it was a battle you could have won. But somewhere along the way, you lost your chance. The American forces will regroup. Hopefully, someone else will succeed where you failed.

THE END

To follow another path, turn to page 10.
To learn more about the War of 1812, turn to page 101.

You don't hesitate. "Let's attack," you say, confidently.

Perry smiles and slaps you on the shoulder. "Full ahead," he calls out. The sails billow as the *Niagara* cuts through the waves, right into the heart of the British fleet. "Fire!"

Master Commandant Perry (right) at the Battle of Lake Erie

Turn the page.

Your charge catches the British unaware. You come at them broadside, that way you can target the entire side of each ship. Your guns fire away, blasting into the British ships over and over.

The attack is a success! The broken British fleet has no choice but to surrender.

The men on the *Niagara* let out a loud cheer. Thanks to your efforts, you've regained control of Lake Erie. It's a crushing blow to the British efforts. The U.S. forces are one big step closer to winning the War of 1812.

THE END

To follow another path, turn to page 10.
To learn more about the War of 1812, turn to page 101.

You can't resist the chance to use the British cannons against them.

"Come on!" you call, charging out into the opening. Ezekiel hesitates but follows you.

The enemy spots you and opens fire. But you're already across the clearing and ducking for cover behind the cannons before they can find their range.

Turn the page.

Ezekiel, however, isn't so lucky. He's only a few steps from safety when a shot catches him in the gut. You scream as he falls to the ground. He's not moving at all.

In a rage, you swivel the cannons to fire on the enemy position. But while the cannons were abandoned, there are no cannonballs here. They're useless!

The sound of battle is all around you, but you are trapped and useless in the clearing. Your friend lies dead because of a decision you made.

The Americans win the Battle of the Thames. But not because of you. You wanted action. You never imagined that you'd be so useless when it finally came.

THE END

To follow another path, turn to page 10.
To learn more about the War of 1812, turn to page 101.

The British forces are in chaos. The Battle of the Thames is an overwhelming victory for the Americans.

It's a crushing defeat for the British, and even more for the American Indians. With Tecumseh dead, his coalition of American Indian forces falls apart.

You remain with General Harrison for much of the war, becoming one of his most trusted men. When the war is over and the Americans have defeated the British, Harrison becomes an American hero.

Nearly 30 years later, he's elected president. He remembers the men loyal to him. He invites you to join him in Washington, D.C., as a member of his White House staff.

Turn the page.

While Ezekiel was as brave a soldier as you, being Black means life is more difficult than yours. He faces racism and is offered fewer opportunities than you.

Eventually, Ezekiel starts a small farm in western Pennsylvania. It's not easy, but he makes it work. Years later, as old men, you still get together and relive the memory of your victory at the Battle of the Thames.

THE END

To follow another path, turn to page 10.
To learn more about the War of 1812, turn to page 101.

CHAPTER 3

CHOOSING SIDES

General Andrew Jackson sits tall on his horse barking out orders. You have mixed feelings as you look at the man. You're half Creek on your mother's side. Jackson led forces against your people in what has been called the Creek War—a part of the larger War of 1812.

The war has divided the Creek people. Some see the war as a way to fight back against increasing American settlement in Creek lands. Others feel that working with the United States is the better choice. Many Creek people have taken up arms to fight the British forces. You are one of them.

Turn the page.

Andrew Jackson

It's a difficult position. In many cases, you're fighting against your own people. You disagree with their decision to support the British in the war. But they're still your people.

"Snap out of it," says your best friend, Micco. He smacks you playfully on the back of your head.

You grin. It's not the first time he's caught you lost in thought. Micco is your complete opposite. You're a thinker—careful and deliberate. Micco is impulsive. He follows his instincts. Perhaps your differences are what make you a good team.

You turn your attention back to Jackson. He says that enemy forces are gathering to your south. A big battle may be coming. You know that in this case, the enemy is a band of Creek called the Red Sticks.

Turn the page.

While you support the United States, the Red Sticks feel that the nation is expanding too quickly and invading their lands. They have joined the British in hopes of slowing down that expansion.

Red Stick raids have bothered colonists in the Mississippi Territory—present-day Alabama—since the start of the war. Jackson wants to put the raids to an end.

You shake your head. "I wish none of this was happening," you say. But Micco doesn't even hear you. His focus is on Jackson, who is ordering troop movements to prepare for battle.

"You two, head south," orders your commanding officer. "Scout the area. We need to know what we're up against. How many men? What's their exact position? Are they on the move?"

"Yes sir," you respond. You and Micco aren't really fighters. You're scouts. You know the land, and you're perfectly suited for the job.

"Should we ride?" Micco asks. He loves horses and is an excellent rider.

Going on horseback will give you speed. But you can move with a lot more stealth on foot. What's more important to you right now?

- To go on horseback, turn to page 50.
- To head out on foot, turn to page 52.

You can't resist the chance to head out on horseback. You and Micco mount up and head south. You ride a brown mare called Sally. She's a sure-footed horse.

You move along the Tallapoosa River into the heart of Red Stick territory. On horseback, you make good time. As you draw nearer to the enemy camp, Micco starts to pull ahead.

"Slow down," you warn. But Micco is eager. He presses on—too fast for your taste.

It proves to be a big mistake. Suddenly, a musket shot rings out. "We've been spotted," you call.

You pull up, scanning the woods around you. Several figures emerge in front of you. Your heart sinks as you notice others moving in from either side. You know without looking that more Red Stick fighters are closing in from behind.

You're surrounded. Micco's horse lets out a loud whinny. Sally stands quietly, waiting for you to tell her what to do.

One of the men in front of you calls out. "Lay down your weapons."

Creek Indians

- To do as you're told, turn to page 54.
- To fight, turn to page 60.

You shake your head.

"We need to do this on foot," you say. "Horses would be faster, but they'd make us a lot easier to spot too."

Micco slumps his shoulders, but he doesn't question your decision. You're the more experienced scout, and acting impulsively has backfired on him before. He trusts your judgment.

You pack a bit of food and canteens of water and head out. Your journey takes you along the course of the Tallapoosa River, which winds through Mississippi Territory.

It's spring, and the land is fresh and green with new growth. The smell of blooming orchids fills the air, and the singing of birds leaves you feeling right at home. You use a small tarp to set up a camp for the night.

The next day, you enter the heart of enemy territory. "Do you see that?" Micco asks, pointing.

It's a small dirt path that cuts through the hilly woods. Following it would make your journey a lot easier. But it could be dangerous if the enemy uses it.

- To take the path, turn to page 56.
- To steer clear of it, turn to page 58.

"Do it," you tell Micco. "We're surrounded. We have no choice."

You toss your weapons to the ground and slowly dismount. One of the enemy warriors grabs Sally's reigns. He can't be more than 15 years old

Another much older man steps forward.

"You are Creek," he says.

You nod.

"Why do you fight for the Americans?" he asks. "They steal our land. They destroy everything. All we want is to keep our homes and stop their endless expansion. You are a traitor to your own people."

You know the Americans steal Creek lands, but if America win this war, you'll be better off than if you fight with the British and lose.

You don't think these men will appreciate you saying that. You remain silent and simply shake your head.

"Join us," says the man. "It's not too late to fight on the right side. What do you say?

- To join the Red Sticks, turn to page 62.
- To refuse, turn to page 64.

You look up and down the dirt path. It's completely empty.

"Let's go," you tell Micco, "Just be careful."

For the next hour, you follow the dirt path through the wilderness. You don't see a sign of people.

"We're deep in Red Stick territory now," you whisper. "If you see anything—"

An arrow whizzes past your face. It slams into the trunk of a nearby tree. A second arrow follows. It strikes just inches below the first.

You stop and hold your breath. Your heart races. You realize that those were warning shots.

Micco turns and runs into the trees, back in the direction that you came from. Your first instinct is to run as well. But you're supposed to be a warrior. Is that the brave choice?

William Weatherford, or Red Eagle, a part-Creek warrior who fought on the side of the U.S. in the War of 1812

Your gun is strapped to your back. You could reach for it now. A musket might make any attackers think twice.

- To run, turn to page 65.
- To go for your weapon, turn to page 67.

You shake your head.

"A path will be watched. We'd be walking into a death trap."

You press on. The wooded, hilly terrain is difficult to navigate. The river twists and bends, forcing you off course again and again.

Just when you start to think you've gone the wrong way, you hear distant voices. Slowly, you creep forward. A steep hillside stands before you. At the top is a barricade made of earth and logs. One young man stands on top of the hill. He's a lookout.

"Stay back," you whisper. You and Micco both duck behind tree trunks.

As you watch, you spot more figures moving about above. "This is it," you whisper. "It's the Red Stick camp."

"How many do you think there are?" Micco asks.

That's what your commanders will want to know too. But there's no way to tell from down here. The camp sits above, blocked from view. From a distance, you can hear children's voices. It's no simple camp. This is a settlement.

"Let's go up where we can get a better view," Micco says. He starts to move out from behind his tree.

"Wait," you call. "Let's think before we move."

You have to get higher if you want to get a sense of their numbers, but you already have important information. You know the location and the terrain of the enemy's defenses. Should you risk your lives to climb the hill and learn even more?

- To return to camp with what you know, turn to page 68.
- To climb the hillside to learn more, turn to page 70.

You grab your musket. Micco takes the cue and does the same. He fires a shot into the woods. It's a warning. For all his bravado, Micco would never shoot a fellow Creek.

You know that warning shots won't be enough to scare them away. You dig your heels in, telling Sally to charge. You ride toward the enemy, weapon in hand. Maybe the sudden action will catch the enemy off guard. You let out a battle cry, holding your musket in the air.

It's a hopeless and foolish charge. An arrow whizzes your way. It catches Sally on the upper part of one of her front legs. The horse rears back, throwing you from your saddle.

You crash to the ground with a thud. Your gun slips from your hand and falls out of reach. You grab for the knife that you keep in your boot, then scramble to your feet.

Another arrow whizzes through the air. This one catches you in the left shoulder. It spins you around, but you stay on your feet. You run, but another arrow catches you in the leg. Moments later, a third strikes. The enemy is closing in all around you.

You slump down to the mossy dirt. You can hear Micco fall from his horse as he tries to flee. This is going to end badly for both of you. Your part in the War of 1812 is at an end.

THE END

To follow another path, turn to page 10.
To learn more about the War of 1812, turn to page 101.

You pause for a moment, weighing your options. Refusing him now will probably cost you your life. And he makes some good points about how Americans are taking over Native lands. Maybe you've been fighting on the wrong side of this all along.

"We will join you," you finally reply. You speak for Micco as well, hoping he won't argue. Luckily, he doesn't.

The man introduces himself as Menawa. He leads you back to their camp on the top of a steep hillside. It's surrounded by a barricade made of earth and logs.

For several days, you help prepare for battle. When Jackson and his troops finally come, the battle is long and brutal. The Red Sticks hold off the U.S. troops for hours. But they are outgunned and outmanned.

You and Micco charge into battle, as a group of U.S. soldiers breech the defensive wall. You fight bravely, a soldier's bayonet catches you. Micco rushes to your side. But there's nothing he can do. Already, the world is fading away.

THE END

To follow another path, turn to page 10.
To learn more about the War of 1812, turn to page 101.

Neamathla, leader of the Red Stick Creeks

You stare the man in the eyes. You suspect he doesn't want to kill you. But you believe that you're fighting for the right side.

"I'm sorry," you say in a soft voice. "I can't do that."

A look of sadness washes over the man's face. He looks at the ground and shakes his head.

"Then you are lost," he says. "I'm sorry. But we cannot let you go. And I have no interest in prisoners. You give me no choice."

You know what's coming. When you agreed to fight in this war, you knew it might cost you your life.

THE END

To follow another path, turn to page 10.
To learn more about the War of 1812, turn to page 101.

There's no way this is just one enemy warrior. There could easily be a dozen in the trees all around you. Fighting is pointless.

You turn and run, following Micco north. Branches slap at your face. You almost trip over a big tree root that juts out from the ground.

With every second that passes, you expect an arrow to hit you. But none do. The enemy seems content just to chase you away.

You catch up to Micco and run away as quickly as you can.

"Let's get back to camp," he says. "We can at least report that the enemy is patrolling the area. That's better than nothing, right?"

You nod silently. But you know that's not the kind of intelligence your commanders were wanting when they sent you.

Turn the page.

Your information will be helpful, but you can't help but feel you're going back a failure. Sure, you know where the Red Sticks are stationed, but you don't know how to help your fellow soldiers prepare for battle. Perhaps life as a scout just isn't for you.

THE END

To follow another path, turn to page 10.
To learn more about the War of 1812, turn to page 101.

With a quick, smooth movement, you grab your gun and swing it out in front of you.

"Show yourself!" you shout into the woods.

A figure emerges from behind a tree. Then another. And another. Your heart sinks. You're surrounded.

Arrows whiz through the air. But these aren't warning shots. And they don't miss their target. You should have followed Micco. Maybe then the enemy would have let you live.

THE END

To follow another path, turn to page 10.
To learn more about the War of 1812, turn to page 101.

Part of you wants to keep going. But it's not the smart decision. You'll be exposed and defenseless while climbing the hillside.

You already know that the enemy has a watch posted. You could probably avoid the sentry you spotted, but he may not be the only one.

"No," you tell Micco. "We can't risk it. We know the exact location of the enemy. We have a sense of their defenses. We have to get this information back."

Micco sighs before giving a small nod. Silently, you back away from the settlement, careful to stay in the deepest part of the woods.

The trek back takes another full day. But you return to your camp and report what you've seen.

"Good work," says one of the officers.

Another officer pipes in and says, "We're planning an attack soon. We'll wipe those Red Sticks right off the map."

You did your part. The battle that follows is brutal. The Red Sticks are crushed. You can't help but feel a sense of sadness that so many Creek were cut down. But you chose your side, and you did your job. From where you stand, there is no real winning side in this war.

THE END

To follow another path, turn to page 10.
To learn more about the War of 1812, turn to page 101.

You hesitate. Is it a good idea to get closer?

Micco is ready to go. His enthusiasm convinces you to press forward.

It's a long, slow climb. You stay low, crawling on all fours through the dirt and mud. As you climb higher, voices filter down through the trees. You can hear men, women, and children.

The barricade is nearby. If you can peek over the edge, you might get a good sense of the enemy's strength. You inch forward, trying to stay silent.

Micco is in front of you. He reaches the barricade first. But as he reaches for a handhold to pull himself to the top, he pulls a large stick loose. It crashes down the slope, slamming into a tree with a loud CRACK!

Suddenly, a commotion erupts from above. A head pops up from the other side of the barricade. Then another, and another.

You've been spotted! Enemy warriors raise their bows to take aim at you. You pushed too far. And now you're going to pay the price.

THE END

To follow another path, turn to page 10.
To learn more about the War of 1812, turn to page 101.

Creek and U.S. forces face off during the Battle of Horseshoe Bend in 1814.

CHAPTER 4

WASHINGTON ON FIRE

The clouds hang low in the sky as you stand on top of the White House roof. It's August of 1814, and Washington, D.C., is in a panic.

Below you, streams of people flee the city. Only miles away, thousands of British soldiers are marching toward the capital. Only a handful of poorly trained militia stand between you and the enemy. The boom of cannon fire echoes in the distance.

Turn the page.

"Can you see anything?" you ask. First Lady Dolley Madison stands before you. She leans out over a railing, peering through a spyglass.

She shakes her head. "Not yet," she answers. "But I'm sure our men will push back the British."

Just then, a messenger brings a note to the rooftop. Madison nods to you to take the note. As one of her top aides, she trusts you.

You glance down at the note. "It's from the president," you say. You feel a chill as you read the note. "He says we should leave the city immediately. The British will be here soon. We cannot let them capture you."

The first lady stands perfectly still. Ever since the British landed at the mouth of the Patuxent River, just 35 miles away, she has insisted that Washington, D.C., will be all right. But that hope is gone now.

Finally, she steps back from the railing. "Well, let's get going," she says. "There is much to do."

Madison suspects what is coming. The British will be relentless. They will probably burn the city.

"We have to save everything we can," she says.

You, several other aides, and the first lady work together to pack up silk drapes, artwork, and more.

When it's finally time to leave, Madison leads you through the state dining room. She pauses, staring up at the wall.

"What is it, ma'am?" asks Paul Jennings, a Black man enslaved by the president.

Madison points at a large painting of George Washington. "We can't let the British destroy it," she insists. "Take it down, please." Unfortunately, the painting's frame is attached to the wall, and you don't have any tools to remove it.

Turn the page.

Dolley Madison directs staff to save George Washington's portrait.

"Do whatever it takes. Just get it to safety," she says.

"We'll get it down," you assure her. "Don't worry. You're running out of time. Please, it's time for you to go."

You stay behind to help. Without tools, all you can do is break the frame and pry the painting loose.

A friend of the first lady rushes through the room on her way out. "Mrs. Madison has more boxes at the residence. Someone needs to get them," she says. "Hurry!"

The British are entering the city. Chaos is breaking out all around.

Jennings looks to you for instructions. Should you take the painting? Or should you go get the boxes?

- To take the painting, turn to page 78.
- To go back for the boxes, turn to page 80.

You grab the painting. "I'll get this out of here," you say.

Jennings nods. "Good. I'll check the residence. Good luck."

"You too," you reply.

With that, you head out. Madison is probably already long gone. But several horses are still standing outside. With the sounds of battle all around you, you claim one of the horses—a large brown stallion. A small fruit cart stands not far from the post. You grew up on a farm, so it's an easy job for you to hitch up the cart, which is large enough to hold the big painting. A black tarp lies inside the cart. You cover the painting with it before riding away.

It's not your horse or your cart. But you're acting on the orders of the first lady. You hope the owners will understand.

Dust kicks up as you urge the horse out onto the streets. British troops are swarming the city. You can't risk getting caught. The British are advancing from the east. You could ride west, to the banks of the Potomac River. Or you could head north.

The British attack on Washington, D.C., 1814

- To ride west toward the river, turn to page 82.
- To ride north, turn to page 93.

"There are other wagons being loaded outside," you tell Jennings. "Find someone you can trust. Tell them to get the painting to safety. I'll go back up to the residence."

Jennings nods and heads out with the painting.

"Be careful, Paul," you call out.

He's a good man, and you have the sudden fear that you may never see him again. "Get yourself somewhere safe."

With that, you head back toward the residence. People rush through the hallways, carrying cases, boxes, and important papers. A blast of cannon fire rocks the building, shaking the walls and leaving your ears ringing.

"They're here!" someone shouts. "The British are here! They're setting everything on fire!"

You rush through the chaos, determined to get whatever Madison had packed away. But when you get to the residence, all you see is boxes of fine china—plates, dishes, platters, and more. You shake your head. It's valuable, but you couldn't save it now if you tried. Not with so much danger all around you. It's too heavy. You turn around and rush out.

Smoke begins to billow into the halls. You could jump out of a nearby window. You're on the ground level, so it would be easy to flee the building. But that won't get you to a horse or carriage, and that's what you need in order to flee the city. If you can get to the back of the building, there might be time to find a horse. But you'd have to go through the smoke.

- To exit through a window, turn to page 83.
- To risk running through the smoke, turn to page 87.

West seems like the safest direction. You move along the city streets to the banks of the Potomac River. Several ships and boats are launching, getting clear of the city.

You pull up and scan the water. A man is loading gear into a small boat. "Hello there," you call out.

The man waves. "I never thought Washington, D.C., could fall to the British," he says. "But I'm no fool. I know when I'm wrong. You should get out while there's still time. I'm headed to my brother's farm. I'll wait out the battle there. Here's hoping our troops can take the city back."

The man seems like a patriot. Could he keep the painting safe? Part of you thinks it's a good idea. But giving such an important piece of American history to a random stranger feels odd. Is it really a good idea?

- To keep the painting, turn to page 96.
- To send it with the man, turn to page 98.

The building is on fire. You have to get out any way you can. You rush to the nearest window, throw it open, and launch yourself through. You come down on your shoulder. Ignoring the pain, you roll and spring to your feet. You run from the building as fast as you can.

Thick black smoke rises up all around you. In the distance, British redcoats move through the streets of Washington.

You can hardly believe what you're seeing. They're destroying the city. No one is safe.

You jog down the streets, away from the fires and the British troops. As you reach an intersection, a group of British soldiers appear about a block away. They don't spot you right away. You're in serious trouble if they do.

Turn the page.

British troops burning the White House

You take shelter in an unlocked cellar for the night. Fires burn throughout the next day. British troops flood the streets.

You hide for most of the day. Late that afternoon, you peak out when you hear thunder.

To the west, a wall of heavy, dark clouds light up with flashes of lightning. The clouds block out the sun, casting the city in a strange darkness, tinted orange and black by the still-burning buildings.

As the storm bears down, a dark funnel reaches down from the cloud toward the ground.

"Tornado!" you whisper, in horror.

Just then, a group of about a dozen British troops emerge from around a corner. They see you.

The storm closes in from one direction. British troops are bearing down on you from the other. Fires burn all around you.

- To run away from the tornado toward the British, turn to page 86.

- To flee the British troops toward the tornado, turn to page 89.

The approaching tornado sounds like a freight train. You take off running—away from the tornado, but toward the British troops.

They see it too. Suddenly, they don't seem to care about you at all. They run just as fast as you do.

Torrents of rain dump down on the city. The streets grow muddy and slick. The fires all around the city begin to blink out.

You hear the tornado is closing in. Debris whips up all around you. Something sharp slams into your leg, but you ignore the pain.

To your left, a low drainage ditch lies alongside the road. To your right, the door to a small shop blows open and closed in the wind. Which place should you take shelter?

- To lie in the drainage ditch, turn to page 91.
- To dive into the shop, turn to page 92.

Your only chance to get out of both the house *and* the city is to head into danger. You take a deep breath and charge toward the smoke. If you can make it to the end of the hallway, turn left, and get to a rear door, there's a good chance you can get a ride out of here.

The smoke thickens. As you reach the end of the hallway, your eyes sting. You can barely see where you're going.

To the right, an orange glow flickers. Flames are consuming the walls, carpet, and furniture. A blast of heat washes over you.

Suddenly, you feel faint. Your head is spinning. Confused, you lose your sense of direction. You stumble toward the fire before realizing your mistake.

Turn the page.

You double over, coughing. As you gasp for breath, smoke fills your lungs. You fall to the floor. The distant sound of panicked voices and cracking flames slowly fades away as the world goes dark. You just hope the first lady made it out in time, because your adventure ends here.

THE END

To follow another path, turn to page 10.
To learn more about the War of 1812, turn to page 101.

You don't know where the tornado is going. But you are sure that the British soldiers will come for you. With that in mind, you run toward the funnel cloud.

The wind howls as the tornado approaches. The rain falls so heavily that you can't even see the twister anymore. You only know it's close by the sound of it.

A tornado touching down

Turn the page.

A huge gust of wind sweeps you off your feet. Nearby, wooden boards rip off a building. One of them slams into your shoulder and bounces off your head. The world goes dark.

When you regain consciousness, the storm has passed. Somehow, you're alive. But you've lost a lot of blood. You need help.

The British find you. They have a reputation for being brutal, even toward civilians. But perhaps the shared experience of the storm has softened them. They bandage your wounds and let you go.

You look out on the streets of Washington. Your city is in shambles. But the worst is over. When the war is over, all of this will need to be rebuilt. You plan to be here to help.

THE END

To follow another path, turn to page 10.
To learn more about the War of 1812, turn to page 101.

Every fiber of your being tells you to get inside. But in a tornado, the key is to get as low as you can. You dive into the drainage ditch. You lie facedown in the mud, using your arms to cover your head.

The twister is just seconds behind you. The sound is overwhelming. The wind and suction almost lift you up. It lasts less than a minute. When the twister has passed, you slowly stand up.

The pouring rain is putting out most of the city's fires. The violent storm has hit the British hard. Their time setting fires is probably over.

Washington has survived. You have too. Your next task will be looking for survivors.

THE END

To follow another path, turn to page 10.
To learn more about the War of 1812, turn to page 101.

Your first instinct is to get inside. You charge for the door and burst into the shop. It's empty. Tools, canned food, and other supplies line the small store's shelves. You duck behind the counter as the wind howls.

You don't have to wait long. The tornado hits the building with incredible force. The deadly storm crushes the walls and sends everything in the shop—including you—flying brutally through the air. You have no hope of survival.

The tornado saves Washington. The rain puts out the fires, while the violent storm crushes the British troops. But none of that will do you any good. Luck just wasn't on your side this time.

THE END

To follow another path, turn to page 10.
To learn more about the War of 1812, turn to page 101.

You turn to the north and ride. To the east, buildings are on fire. You can see large groups of British redcoats advancing through the city. They seem determined to completely destroy the capital. They want to break the will of the American people.

"Well, I can't stop that," you mumble to yourself. "But I can save this one small part of our history."

For a few minutes, you think you might make it. If you can get to the countryside, you can find a farmhouse to store the painting. But as you reach the outskirts of the city, a group of British soldiers spots you. Two of them step out into the road, guns in hand.

"Stop!" one of them orders. "Where do you think you're going?"

Turn the page.

"Back to my farm," you lie. "I had a cart of fruit for sale. I'm not part of this war. Please, let me pass. I have no disagreement with the Crown."

The man laughs. He looks you up and down. "Those are not the clothes of a farmer. By the way you're dressed, I'd say you've got something other than fruit in that cart. How about we have a look? If there's fruit in there, I'll let you go. Anything else . . . well, lying to a British soldier during war will cost you your life."

Helplessly, you watch the men throw back the tarp. What they find surprises them.

"Well look at this!" a soldier says, holding up the painting.

"George Washington? That traitor! I think we should use the painting for target practice!"

The men are so distracted that nobody is watching you. You take a chance, digging your heels into the horse's side and shouting a command. The horse takes off at a full speed down the road.

The soldiers scramble. One gets off a shot at you. But you're already out of range. You ride at full speed until Washington, D.C., is long out of sight.

You failed to save the painting. But at least you made it out alive.

THE END

To follow another path, turn to page 10.
To learn more about the War of 1812, turn to page 101.

"Good luck," you call out. You watch the man leave, disappearing around a bend in the river.

Was it a mistake to hold on to the painting? Who knows what could have happened to it with a stranger. You hope you made the right decision.

You ride north. As you ride, dark clouds gather to the west. Soon, rumbles of thunder warn of a coming storm.

You're far out of the city, in a remote countryside. You search for a place to take shelter, but the storm is coming fast. Soon, sheets of rain are pouring down over you. Wind howls.

Your horse is spooked by the weather. He tries to bolt. But all he does is tip over the fruit cart that holds the precious painting. Everything spills out.

The painting falls in a muddy puddle. You grab for it, desperately trying to keep it safe. But in the torrents of rain, it's hopeless. You can only watch as this precious piece of American history is destroyed.

You survived the British attack on Washington, D.C. But you failed to protect the painting of Washington. You know the first lady will be very disappointed.

THE END

To follow another path, turn to page 10.
To learn more about the War of 1812, turn to page 101.

You need to get the painting out of the city. You'll just have to take a chance on this stranger.

"Can I ask you a favor?" you call out.

You explain what's happening. The man, whose name is Alexander, quickly agrees.

"Anything for the first lady," he says. "I'll store it in the back of my brother's barn. Nobody will ever look there. And when this all blows over, I'll return it to the president. You have my word."

You help the man load the painting and watch as he disappears around a bend in the river.

You ride north, leaving the city behind. You head to Philadelphia, where you have family.

Later, you reconnect with Dolley Madison. You're by her side as the United States wins the war. And true to his word, Alexander returns the painting. You smile as workers hang it back up.

It was a terrible war, and Washington, D.C., suffered a huge price. But the nation will rebuild.

THE END

To follow another path, turn to page 10.
To learn more about the War of 1812, turn to page 101.

Gilbert Stuart's portrait of President George Washington, saved during the War of 1812

CHAPTER 5

RETURN TO THE BATTLEFIELDS

In 1783, the United States earned its independence by defeating Great Britain in the American Revolution. The young nation was just beginning its struggles, however. As it expanded ever westward, it spread out over the lands of Native peoples, causing constant conflict.

The rapid growth threatened Great Britain's claims in North America, especially Canada. The British grew more and more uneasy with U.S. expansion.

In the early 1800s, Britain imposed trade restrictions on the United States. It blockaded ports. It seized American ships and forced American sailors to serve in the British military. It also sided with many Native peoples who fought to protect their lands and slowed U.S. expansion.

Many U.S. leaders and citizens still held bitter feelings toward Great Britain from the colonial period and the American Revolution. Some felt that Britain was bullying the young nation.

In 1812, tempers boiled over. The United States declared war on Great Britain. The War of 1812 had begun.

Great Britain responded with force. It made agreements with Native peoples all along the edge of the expanding nation. Meanwhile, British soldiers sailed to the United States.

Neither side found the easy victory for which they had hoped. Great Britain took control of the north early on, but American forces fought back and reclaimed most of the ground it had lost. American forces led attacks on Native peoples aligned with Great Britain, often treating the enemy with shocking brutality.

As the war dragged on, British raids along coasts grew more violent. On August 24, 1814, the British reached Washington, D.C. They quickly began to burn the city.

British forces attacking Washington, D.C., 1814

A powerful storm rolled through the city the next day, complete with a tornado. The storm system was largely responsible for putting out the fires and saving the city.

Eventually, both sides grew tired of the fighting. They began to negotiate a peace treaty in the European nation of Belgium, which had remained neutral in the war.

The Battle of New Orleans, 1815, the final battle of the War of 1812

In late 1814, they agreed to end the war. But news travelled slowly in those days. The fighting continued into 1815, before word reached the commanders in the field.

Both sides claimed victory in the war. Most military historians call it a draw, with neither side winning. Still, the War of 1812 helped shape politics in the United States for generations. The American-claimed victory over the powerful British sparked a wave of nationalism in the United States that hadn't been seen since the end of the Revolutionary War.

The end of the war also marked the beginning of the downfall of the powerful Federalist Party, which had opposed the war.

Finally, the war prompted the United States to become more active in international politics. This is a stance that the country has maintained into the modern day.

Timeline of the War of 1812

November 7, 1811
William Henry Harrison leads U.S. forces to victory over Tecumseh's Confederacy in the Battle of Tippecanoe. The battle sets the stage for further fighting in the War of 1812.

June 18, 1812
The United States declares war on Great Britain. The War of 1812 begins.

July 12, 1812
U.S. General William Hull leads U.S. forces into British-held Canada.

August 15-16, 1812
The British attack Detroit, forcing U.S. forces to surrender the city.

August 30, 1813
U.S. naval forces earn a victory in the Battle of Lake Erie.

October 5, 1813
U.S. forces defeat Tecumseh's Confederacy in the Battle of the Thames. Tecumseh is killed in the fighting.

March 2, 1814
Andrew Jackson leads U.S. forces to victory over the Red Sticks in the Battle of Horseshoe Bend.

August 24, 1814
British forces enter Washington, D.C., and set the city on fire. A storm the next day helps to put out the flames.

December 24, 1814
The Treaty of Ghent is signed, with both sides agreeing to end the war.

January 8, 1815
U.S. forces defeat the British in the Battle of New Orleans. News of the Treaty of Ghent did not arrive in time to stop the battle.

Other Paths to Explore

1. Native peoples fought on both sides in the War of 1812. Imagine you were a Native person choosing a side in the war. How might that feel? Would you be angry with those who chose the other side? Or would you understand?

2. Many Americans set out west, looking for new land and opportunities. They didn't often consider the Native peoples who already lived there. How would you feel as an American, moving into territory where you are not wanted?

3. In the South, enslaved people watched as the British marched toward Washington. The British opposed slavery, but they also brought violence and destruction. If you were an enslaved person, how would you have felt about their arrival?

Bibliography

American Battlefield Trust: War of 1812
battlefields.org/learn/war-1812

Hickey, Donald R. *The War of 1812: A Forgotten Conflict.*
Urbana, Ill.: University of Illinois Press, 2012.

History: War of 1812
history.com/topics/war-of-1812/war-of-1812

Watson, Robert P. *America's First Crisis: The War of 1812.*
New York: State University of New York Press, 2014.

Winkler, John F. *The Thames 1813: The War of 1812 on the
Northwest Frontier.* Oxford: Osprey Publishing, 2016.

Zielinski. Sarah, "The Tornado That Saved Washington,"
Smithsonian Magazine, August 25, 2010. smithsonianmag.
com/science-nature/the-tornado-that-saved-
washington-33901211/

Glossary

barricade (BA-ruh-kade)—a man-made physical barrier

blockade (blok-AYD)—to physically block something, such as a port or waterway, by placing warships all around it

confederation (kuhn-fed-dur-AY-shuhn)—a group of nations or peoples who unite for a common cause

enlist (in-LIST)—to join the military

flagship (FLAG-ship)—the ship that carries the captain of the fleet

fleet (FLEET)—a large group of ships

militia (muh-LISH-uh)—a civilian fighting unit, which isn't a part of the military

musket (MUHSS-kit)—a gun with a long barrel that was used before the rifle was invented

rations (RA-shuhns)—a set amount of food allotted to a person each day

retreat (ri-TREET)—to fall back from battle

seize (SEEZ)—to take something by force

sentry (SEN-tree)—a guard

stealth (STELTH)—the ability to move without being detected

Read More

Adams, Simon. *The War of 1812*. New York: Crabtree Publishing, 2018.

Cunningham, Kevin. *The War of 1812*. Lake Elmo, MN: Focus Readers, 2019.

Lewis, Cicely. *The Real History of the White House*. Minneapolis: Lerner Publications, 2023.

Internet Sites

American History for Kids
americanhistoryforkids.com/

Dolley Madison: Britannica Kids
kids.britannica.com/students/article/Dolley-Madison/351340

War of 1812 for Kids
nps.gov/subjects/warof1812/for-kids.htm

About the Author

Matt Doeden is a freelance author and editor from Minnesota. He's written numerous children's books on sports, music, current events, the military, extreme survival, and much more. Doeden began his career as a sports writer before turning to publishing. He lives in Minnesota with his wife and two children.

JOIN OTHER HISTORICAL ADVENTURES WITH MORE YOU CHOOSE SEEKING HISTORY!

YOU CHOOSE
COMING TO AMERICA
THROUGH THE ANGEL ISLAND IMMIGRATION STATION
35 CHOICES 11 ENDINGS

YOU CHOOSE
FIGHTING FOR FREEDOM
ALONG THE UNDERGROUND RAILROAD
37 CHOICES 17 ENDINGS

YOU CHOOSE
SEEKING FORTUNE
DURING THE CALIFORNIA GOLD RUSH
41 CHOICES 18 ENDINGS

YOU CHOOSE
TAKING A STAND
DURING THE WAR OF 1812
39 CHOICES 30 ENDINGS